Old QUEEN'S PARK

by

Eric Eunson

© Copyright Eric Eunson 1995
First Published in the United Kingdom, 1995
By Stenlake Publishing, Ochiltree Sawmill, The Lade, Ochiltree, Ayrshire KA18 2NX
Telephone/Fax: 01290 423114

ISBN 1-872074-51-0

INTRODUCTION

Glasgow historians are divided on the question of whether Queen's Park was named in honour of Queen Victoria or Mary, Queen of Scots. The first part of the public park was officially opened in 1862, Victoria's Silver Jubilee, and it would have been positively treasonous for the city fathers to have honoured another Queen on such an occasion. With streets in the immediate vicinity of the park named after Prince Albert, Prince Edward, and Victoria herself, the pro-Mary theory therefore seems moved more by patriotism than probability.

Historically though, the Victorian park is still strongly linked to Mary, for it contains the last undeveloped fragment of her final battlefield. The Battle of Langside took place on May 13th 1568, and although it was a decisive conflict marking the end of the Queen's reign, it was an unremarkable affair as battles go. The 4,500 strong force of the Regent Moray was assembled around the village of Langside and in the south east corner of the park, which is now a miniature golf course. Mary's larger army of 6,000 gathered on Clincart Hill, presently occupied by Langside College. The fighting began around 9 a.m., and it took the Regent's army just three quarters of an hour to put the Queen's forces to flight. Although outnumbered, the Regent's men were led by more experienced commanders, and the victory was accomplished with the combined loss to both sides of only 300 soldiers. The personalities of Mary's reign and the battle are commemorated in street names throughout the south side of the city; among them her commanders the Lords Herries, Terregles and the Earl of Eglinton; her opponents Moray, Glencairn and Grange; and her husbands Bothwell and Darnley, who even boasts a modern housing scheme!

Among Mary's allies was Sir John Maxwell of Nether Polloc, whose huge estate centred on what is now Pollok Park. Maxwell's lands were confiscated by the Regent after the battle, and handed over to his friend Alexander, Earl of Glencairn, who had been on the winning side. A year later, however, Maxwell was forgiven his loyalty to the Queen, and his lands were restored upon payment of compensation to Glencairn. The Maxwells flourished, and over the ensuing century acquired, through purchase and prudent marriages, an estate that included most of the land from Pollok to the Gorbals.

In 1798 the Maxwells sold Camphill Farm to a Glasgow cotton manufacturer called Robert Thomson. This now forms the western part of Queen's Park. It was bounded on the west, north and south by the present park boundaries; and on the east by Pathead Farm, which extended to the edge of the modern allotments. By 1820 the farms of Camphill and Crossmyloof, on the opposite side of Pollokshaws Road, were the property of James Oswald, a Royal Navy captain resident in Scotstoun. In a manuscript document of that date he confirms a lease of both farms to Robert Crawford of Possil. According to this record, the Crawford family had been feuars of these properties since 1780.

Camphill House was built on the site of the old thatched farm house, but its exact date has been lost. Experts have judged it to date from 1800-18, but Crawford's feu document of 1820 refers only to "the mailling or farm now called the Camphill farm of Langside", and makes no reference to any recently built desirable country seat. The now demolished gate house of Camphill was described as "new" in 1831, so it seems probable that the true date of the house lies between 1820-30.

The remaining part of the present park was the farm of Pathead, which remained in Maxwell hands until 1830, when Neale Thomson, the owner of Camphill, exchanged the farm for some acres Maxwell was keen to acquire at Crossmyloof. In 1847 Thomson founded a bread bakery at Crossmyloof, and soon he was supplying thousands of loaves to the city daily. In 1857 he sold the 143 acre Pathead farm for £30,000 to Glasgow Corporation, who intended to turn it into a new suburban park.

Public opinion branded the plan a white elephant, as the chosen site was in open country, fully a mile from the southern boundary of the city. Joseph Paxton, designer of the Crystal Palace, was invited to submit plans for the layout of the park. Paxton's plans included a huge glass winter garden to house concerts and exhibitions, and a man made lake. These attractions were considered too extravagant, and the plans were modified by the City Master of Works, John Carrick. Coincidentally, Paxton had also been invited to submit plans for Kelvingrove Park in 1854, and on that occasion too Carrick edited out a lake and winter gardens! The park was constructed by the unemployed during 1858-59, and was formally opened on September 11th 1862.

The creation of Queen's Park was anticipated to stimulate development around its margins, and Carrick also prepared plans for a street layout on its northern edge in 1860. He laid out Victoria Road, a wide new boulevard aligned with the main gate of the park, and envisioned a series of elegant squares and terraces branching from it. He also stipulated that all churches in the new district were to be built with spires. Development around the park was steady but undramatic, and it was not until around 1900 that the last of Carrick's street plan was built. Developers tended to favour sites in the established suburb of Pollokshields. Feuing there had been started by Sir John Maxwell in 1851, and restrictions he had imposed meant that there was no risk of encroachment by industry. Some limited development of villas had begun in Crosshill in the 1840s. Half a mile to the east of the park, William Dixon began creating the working class burgh of Govanhill in 1870, adjacent to his Govan Iron Works.

In 1866 the trustees of Neale Thomson sold the Camphill estate to Hutcheson's Hospital for £24,000. They feued the ground for building, but plans for houses in the 1870s came to nothing. In 1894 the Corporation bought the 58 acres and mansion house for £60,000 and added them to Queen's Park. By that date the "sandstone jungle" of tenements had already virtually surrounded the park, which is reflected by the enormous increase in the value of the land in less than 20 years, in that pre-inflationary era.

As every Glaswegian knows, or ought to know, the city boasts a greater acreage of green space than any other city in Europe. Queen's Park remains one of the most attractive in the city, by virtue of its maturity (it was Glasgow's third public park); and its varied topography in contrast to other flatter, less well appointed sites. From its highest point at the flagpole, the entire city reveals itself like a relief map, and time can be passed amusingly trying to identify the spires and streets below. The traffic congestion and resulting pollution in the districts around Queen's Park, make it an ever more precious asset to the community.

Eglinton Toll came into being with the upgrading of Pollokshaws Road into a turnpike in 1753. A toll house and weighing machine were built on the site of the St. Andrews Cross gushet building, and remained in service until all road and bridge tolls within Glasgow were abolished in 1874. Until the junction was split by a barrier in 1946, this was said to be the only place in the world where trams travelled in five directions.

4

Mr. Hugh Kennedy at the wheel of his 38 hp. Silent Knight Minerva.

The Kennedy Motor Company was situated in Barrland Street, and from 1907-10 built cars called "Kennedy" and "Ailsa". The Scottish Reliability Trials were organised by the Royal Scottish Automobile Club from 1905-09, and competing cars were put through their paces on a five or six day course including hill climbs, over some of Scotland's most testing roads. The burly man sitting next to Hugh Kennedy is believed to be William McLennan, a pioneer motorist from Orkney. In recent years the garage premises became the police car pound, until the building was pulled down in September 1994.

This photograph was taken in the Coplawhill Tram Depot, and shows cars illuminated in honour of Edward VII's coronation in June 1902. The first part of the depot was built on Pollokshaws Road in 1894, with additions facing Albert Drive between 1899-1912. After Glasgow's last trams ran in 1962, many of the redundant cars were broken up here. Later, part of the depot became an appropriate home to the city's Transport Museum, until this was moved to the Kelvin Hall in the 1980s.

Car 986 was passing the Royal Infirmary en route to Mount Florida, at five o'clock on a foggy Friday night, when it began to accelerate alarmingly. Some passengers later reported hearing a loud bang, and panic began to spread as the speed continued to increase. The driver was flung from his platform near the corner of Stirling Street, and the conductor closed the entrance to the car to prevent terrified passengers from jumping to their injury. Out of control, the car hurtled down the crowded High Street, crashing into two horse drawn lorries outside the College Goods Station. At Ingram Street it ploughed into a cart belonging to G. & C. Moore, Aerated Water manufacturers, killing the horse outright. The van boy, William Heggie of Calton, died the following day from his injuries. It struck another two lorries at the Cross, injuring one horse and one driver. A crowd of men ran after the tram, pursuing it as it sped into the Saltmarket, slowing slightly as the gradient decreased. A young Gorbals man, George Thomas Probert of South Wellington Street, made a heroic leap onto the rear platform, climbed on top of the tram, and knocked the connecting rod off the electric wire. The conductor managed to apply the brake and the battered car came to a halt near Glasgow Green. Although bruised and shaken, none of the passengers were seriously injured. The driver, 45 year old James Dolan of 46 Jamieson Street, Govanhill, suffered severe head injuries and died in the Royal Infirmary the following day. He left a widow and 9 children. This picture was taken in the Coplawhill Depot where the wrecked car had been taken for inspection and repair.

DAMAGED CAR (HIGH St Tram Smash)
JANY 3rd 1908.

Photo By H·C·Glass.

The 18th Glasgow Boys Brigade marching up Pollokshaws Road in the early 1920s. St. Ninian's Church on the left dates from 1872, and was the first Episcopal Church on the south side of the city. The tenements beyond stood on the site of an old hamlet called Muirhouses, which was probably established in the 18th century.

Pte. Wm. Lindsay. Pte. D. Hepburn. Corp. Wm. Bauchop.

Sgt. W. A. Ritchie. Pte. T. Clark.   Pte. T. W. Ness.   Pte. J. C. Smith.   Pte. Wm. Neill.   Pte. R. T. Gibson.
        Col.-Sgt. J. W. Donaldson. Sergt. J. S. Young. Lieut. J. A. Wilkie.   Major D. Yates (G.M.) Lieut. E. Smith. Sergt. Wm. Pillans.
                                Pte. A. Tweedie.   Lce.-Corp. J. Harvey.

W. W. Ingram Photo.

3RD LANARKSHIRE RIFLE VOLUNTEERS.

VICTORIA CHALLENGE SHIELD
WON BY "M" COMPANY (MAJOR D. YATES) 1904.

Members of the 3rd Lanarkshire Rifle Volunteers pictured at the entrance to their drill hall in Coplaw Street. It was built in 1884, and now houses a snooker club. Members of the Rifle Volunteers formed Third Lanark Amateur Football Club in 1872. It was only the fifth club to be formed in Scotland, and was a founder member of the Scottish Football Association. To generations of fans the team was known as the "Hi Hi", the chant of its supporters. After the club was wound up in 1967 some dedicated fans continued to visit its ground, Cathkin Park off Cathcart Road, every Saturday to gaze despondently at the empty pitch.

Hutcheson's Girls Grammar School was founded in 1876, in a building in Elgin Street, Gorbals. It moved to this building in Kingarth Street in the spring of 1912.

Moustaches seem to have been an obligatory accessory to uniform when this picture of the Queens' Park Division of Police was taken in 1903. The police and fire station in Craigie Street were designed in 1892 by the City Surveyor A.B.Macdonald, in a Scottish Baronial style. The fire station was converted into flats in the late 1980s, and the police station has now followed suit with only a small part time office being maintained.

Strathbungo Public School.
Glasgow.

Strathbungo Higher Grade Secondary School was opened in 1894, to accommodate the pupils from the Govanhill and Queen's Park districts who passed the qualifying exam, later called the "11 Plus". The school is now St. John's R.C. Primary, but remains externally unchanged from this 1905 view.

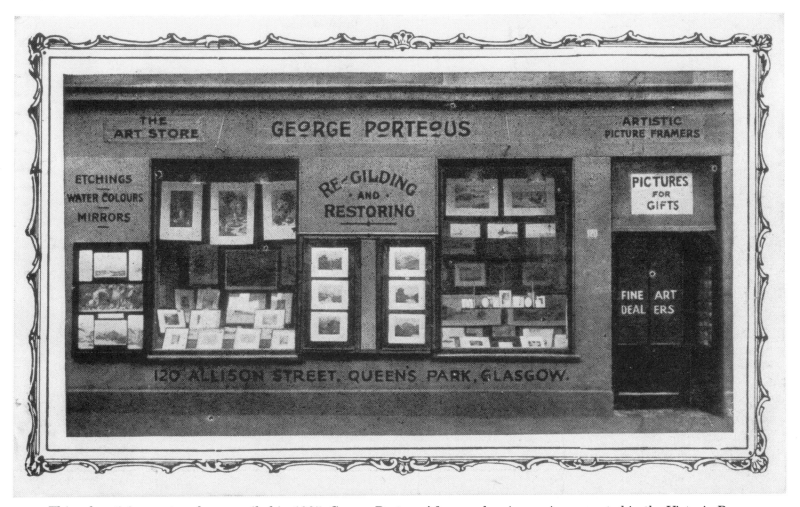

This advertising postcard was mailed in 1935. George Porteous' former shop is now incorporated in the Victoria Bar.

An 1896 view looking south along Pollokshaws Road, to its junction with Allison Street. Within ten years all the quaint old cottages seen here had been demolished and replaced by modern tenements. The village of Strathbungo developed around the junction of these two streets, both of which follow the courses of ancient thoroughfares. By the mid 18th century it was a substantial village with a population of weavers and miners. In 1891 it contained 674 houses and a population of 2,951.

14

Left: Hutchesontown Terrace, at the corner of Prince Edward Street and Niddrie Road under construction in 1896. These were among the last tenements in the area to be built with locally quarried blonde sandstone. Builders switched to pink stone from Ayrshire and Dumfries around 1895.

Right: This photograph of the corner of Allison Street and Pollokshaws Road also dates from 1896.

A "Cunarder" tram in front of Heraghty's bar on Pollokshaws Road in 1954. Horse drawn trams were introduced to Glasgow in 1872 by the Glasgow Tramway and Omnibus Company. By 1880 the lines had reached Pollokshaws and Mount Florida. The Corporation of Glasgow took over the running of the tramways in 1894, and by 1902 had converted the whole system to electric power.

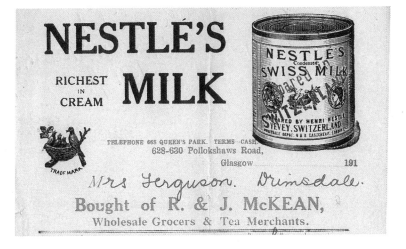

Advertising billheads from 1914. The rice starch and the naptha soap would both have belonged in the laundry. In addition to stiffening fabric, starch also provided it with a light glaze which helped to protect from dirt. The soap bar would have been rubbed onto stubborn stains before washing. Manufacturers have recently implied similar bars are a new innovation!

POLLOKSHAWS ROAD STRATHBUNGO, GLASGOW.

When this 1913 postcard was published, the block in the left foreground was called Regent Park Street, and the block on the right was Bute Terrace. On the skyline is the distinctive tower of the United Free Church, 1888, now sadly derelict. Strathbungo takes its name from a "strath" meaning an area of land beside a stream or river, and "bungo" is most probably a corruption of Mungo, the city's patron saint. There are no streams in the vicinity today that could have been the "Mungo's burn" that the name suggests, but until the 19th century the Kinninghouse Burn flowed immediately to the west of the village.

The Kinninghouse Burn had been completely filled in by 1870, but had its source near Crossmyloof, and entered the Clyde at Kinning Park. It was also served by a tributary that followed roughly the line of the railway cutting that runs below Victoria Road. Old documents also give the name of Strathbungo as Marchtown. "March" is an obsolete word for boundary, and the Kinninghouse Burn marked Lanarkshire's western border with Renfrew. It was also the boundary between the Barony of Gorbals and the lands of the Maxwells of Pollok.

In 1859 Alexander "Greek" Thomson designed the first part of Moray Place, facing onto the Barrhead Railway. It was the first stage of a speculative development by Thomson and his partner James Turnbull, to create a new garden suburb within commuting distance of the city. Regent Park Square, seen here in 1906, followed before 1870, and by 1879 the grid of terraces between Nithsdale Road and Marywood Square had been completed.

A lone car cruises up the middle of Balvicar Street in this 1930 illustration. The former Camphill United Presbyterian Church, on the right, was designed by William Leiper and built between 1875-78. The congregation had to wait another five years until sufficient funds were raised to erect the spire. Niddrie Square, on the left, was formerly called Cromwell Square. The two storey houses on the east side of the square were built in 1895 by Alexander Petrie. The west side was completed in 1900 by John Murray, with a terrace of four storey houses that contained between 7 and 12 apartments.

Queens Park Collegiate, Glasgow. 1946. 55.

This building was erected some time between 1870-8 and was demolished in the 1960s to make way for the Balvicar Centre, facing Niddrie Square. Exact information about the building has proved elusive, but old maps show it as a school. If any reader would like to contact the publisher with more information I will be glad to include it in any future editions of this book.

This well-known Victoria Road institution is not to be confused with the Queen's Park Cafe across the road – not a cafe at all but a pub. It has been the cause of many a failed tryst, with one lovesick punter sitting in the pub, and the other nursing a cold cup of tea in the cafe over the road!

VICTORIA ROAD AND ENTRANCE TO QUEEN'S PARK, GLASGOW.

The building containing the Post Office and the Elim Hall replaced a single storey row of shops in the early 1930s. Next door was the ill-sited Crosshill Cinema, where the soundtrack of films was regularly drowned out by the racket of passing trains.

24

ALBERT DRIVE. QUEEN'S PARK

Albert Drive dates from the late 1860s, and was the first street to be developed west of Victoria Road. It enjoyed an uninterrupted view of the park until the western part of Queen's Drive was built in 1871. The ground floor corner flat, on the right of this 1905 pictures, is now the "Old Vic" pub.

The plain iron gates of the park were replaced by the present pillared art-nouveau entrance in 1907, but otherwise the view down Victoria Road has, structurally at least, scarcely altered. The flamboyant Balmoral Crescent on the right was built between 1884-6.

This wintry vista of Victoria Road from the terrace of Queen's Park dates from around 1910. The site of the terrace gardens was where Paxton's aborted winter gardens were to have stood. Carrick replaced this with a formal garden in an 18th century Dutch style. If the reader wonders what an 18th century Dutch garden looked like, the flower beds are still in their original layout!

Watching the band in Queen's Park in 1908. Most of these old iron bandstands were taken away, along with everyone's railings during the scrap metal drives of the last war. This one, however, was "retired" to the Duchess Park in Motherwell in the early 1920s, where it somehow survived the war and remains to this day. Queen's Park's newly constructed replacement is shown on the facing page, with workmen still landscaping the site in the background.

28

The large, flat area around the bandstand was formerly a marsh, which locals called the "Kirkyard Park" or "De'il's Kirkyard". Tradition had it that the Catholic dead from the Battle of Langside had been buried here as they were denied interment in the Protestant churchyard of Cathcart. In 1831 the wife of the lodge keeper at Camphill reported to the minister that sitting up one night, unable to sleep, she had seen the ghosts of the dead of Langside rise from the mire "amid a sound resembling distant thunder, accompanied by a thin bluish flame of sulphurous origin which momentarily lit up her chamber". When the marsh was drained during the construction of the park no human remains were found.

The park ranger's house in this 1905 view was the old farmhouse of Pathead which was retained when the park was created. Until the 1850s the road from the city to Langside ran in a more or less straight line from the Gorbals, along the route of Langside Road in Crosshill, and ran to the east of the farmhouse, through what are now the bowling green and tennis court.

Queen's Park and much of Langside are situated on a drumlin, which was formed at the end of the ice age, when retreating glaciers deposited soil and rocks which they had scoured up as they advanced. At its highest point the mound rises to 109 feet, and until the mid 18th century it was largely surrounded by moorland and bogs, making it an ideal defensive site. The stones in this 1905 photograph are the most visible remains of a Roman camp, which gave the Camphill Farm its name. It was probably contemporary with the Antonine Wall (c.140 A.D.), and was surrounded by an earth rampart and ditch measuring approximately 120m x100m. Excavations here have uncovered Roman and Medieval remains, and archaeologists have suggested that the earthwork may have been the adaptation by the Romans of an earlier iron age site.

The large boating pond and its smaller ornamental neighbour were excavated out of the lawn of Camphill House in 1905, belatedly echoing Paxton's plans of the 1850s. The path around the pond, from the park's Balvicar Street gate, was the original main drive to the mansion. This 1910 illustration, and other contemporary views, show how popular the pastime of wheeling unhygienically bundled infants around parks was with our Edwardian forebears.

The Camphill hothouses were erected around 1895, and contained a selection of exotic flora and palms set among classical statuary, with a nursery for more sundry plants to replenish the park beds. The photo on the right was sent in 1909, and the lass identified herself as "Mary" who lived at No.1 Allison Street. This conservatory was taken down around 1930, and only the steps on Mary's left and the stump of a sundial now remain. The larger greenhouses facing Battlefield were put up in 1905, and these are now used as propagating houses for all Glasgow's parks.

ENTRANCE TO CAMPHILL PARK, GLASGOW.

E02910

Although documentary evidence does not appear to have survived, experts are in agreement that Camphill House was almost certainly the work of David Hamilton, who lived from 1768-1843. He was one of the city's most celebrated Georgian/early Victorian architects, and his works include Aikenhead House in King's Park; Hutcheson's Hall in Ingram Street; the former Royal Exchange; and the Nelson Obelisk on Glasgow Green. Camphill House was turned into a museum in 1896, and in 1931 attracted an astonishing 101,763 visitors. By 1951 this had fallen to the still impressive figure of 34,000.

The museum latterly included displays of costume and a local exhibition which included items recovered from the battlefield of Langside. When it was closed in the early 1980s, its collection was no doubt consigned to some municipal basement, full of other relics of the city's under represented heritage. For a decade Camphill House was virtually disused, gathering graffiti and looking increasingly sorry for itself. At the time of writing plans are afoot to convert the house into flats, as has been done with the mansions in Tollcross and King's Parks.

Vennard Gardens, Glasgow, S.2

Strathbungo and Crossmyloof retained a distinct boundary of open ground, until the art deco influenced terraces from Vennard Gardens to Titwood Road were built in the late 1920s. This contemporary postcard was published by R.W. Parsons who ran a stationer's shop at 725 Pollokshaws Road.

The maximum height of tenement buildings was fixed at four storeys by the city's Dean of Guild Court in the 1860s. Springhill Gardens, designed in 1904 by John Nisbet, were a rare exception, and five storeys were permitted as the flats faced on to Queen's Park and not other houses. In 1905 Nisbet also designed the nearby art nouveau style Camphill Gate on Pollokshaws Road.

FOUNTAIN & LANGSIDE HALLS, CROSSMYLOOF, GLASGOW.

E02811

The Langside Halls were designed by John Gibson in 1847, and originally stood in Queen Street where they housed the National Bank of Scotland. In 1901 the bank was scheduled to be demolished to make way for a warehouse. The building was bought by the city, moved stone by stone to its present site, and adapted for use as a public hall which opened in 1903. The carving on the facade was executed by John Thomas, who had also worked on the Houses of Parliament. The sculptured heads over the arched windows represent the rivers Clyde, Thames, Severn, Tweed and Humber. The ornate fountain was the work of Robert MacFarlane's Saracen Foundry at Possil, and was typical of examples that the firm exported to every corner of the globe. This one now stands in front of the People's Palace.

A few cottages of old Crossmyloof are on the left of this 1904 picture, but were demolished the following year. In the mid 18th century Crossmyloof consisted of only three cottar houses and a croft, but an 1818 history of Renfrewshire describes it as the most populous village in Cathcart Parish. The writer of this account says "It was, till lately, remarkable chiefly for being the resort of vagrants, who did not conceive themselves to be so little liable to be taken notice of in any place more populous or less obscure. It has become more respectable lately from an increase in the number of its inhabitants who amount to about 500". The Pollokshaws Burgh minutes of 1813 complain that the road through Crossmyloof was troubled by highway robbers.

This view of the head of Minard Road dates from 1904. A public house had existed on the left hand corner since 1817, and was rebuilt as the Corona Bar in 1912. A mosaic in the entrance to the pub depicts a cross lying in the palm of a hand, illustrating the legendary origins of the name of Crossmyloof. The story goes that Mary Queen of Scots passed here in 1568, as she attempted to flee from Castlemilk to Dumbarton. Allegedly, she took her crucifix in her hand and swore "By the cross in my loof (hand) I will be there tonight in spite of yon traitors". Learned historians, however, have established that the queen could not have been here, and that the name of the place is found written at a much earlier date as "Kilmaeldubh" and "Kilmyluc".

The tenements in Minard Road were mostly completed in 1903-5. Note the one legged man on crutches on the left of this 1914 photograph. The low lying area at the foot of the street was once part of an extensive marsh called the Shawmoss, which locals nicknamed the "Honeymugs". The marsh was not completely drained until the 1920s, and had been the source of the Kinninghouse Burn.

Tenements and shops began to spread from Crossmyloof southwards along Pollokshaws Road in the 1860s, and the former village merged into the new district of Shawlands. When Shawlands was annexed by the city in 1891 it contained 567 houses and had a population of 2,660. The handsome Crossmyloof Mansions, at the junction of Kilmarnock and Pollokshaws roads, were built around 1890, and were twenty years old when this postcard was published.

SHAWLANDS CROSS, GLASGOW.

A.5910.

Twenty five years on from the facing photograph, and the cross is still delightfully traffic free. Today pedestrians and motorists are unusually united in their frustration at this congested bottleneck. On the far left of the picture is the Elephant Cinema, which was capped with a model of the eponymous creature. On the right is the ivy clad Shawlands Cross Free Church which was built between 1900-03. Behind this is the Old Shawlands Parish Church, designed by J.A. Campbell and begun in 1885.

Moss Side Road was a country lane in the heart of Shawlands when this postcard was published in 1904. Building did not start here until the erection of the Waverley Cinema in 1923. This was followed by the new Shawlands Academy, begun in 1930.

Kilmarnock Road, Shawlands, Glasgow.

The west side of Kilmarnock Road was first developed with a series of large villas in the 1870s. However, in the early 20th century Shawlands grew in importance as a commercial centre for new, exclusively residential districts such as Newlands. The villas were encroached upon by shops and tenements, and the last of them were demolished in the 1960s to make way for the drab Shawlands Arcade. The shops on the left of this 1930 view date from the mid 1920s. The domed bank in the middle distance was built in 1905 as a branch of the Glasgow Savings Bank.

Bothwell Terrace, Kilmarnock Road in 1908. Many tenement streets used to have blocks with extra names which had been given to them by their builders or owners. As a result of the confusion that this inevitably caused, the Corporation abolished all these extraneous titles in 1923.

The original Shawlands Academy was designed by James Hamilton in 1893, and was about twelve years old when this picture was taken. When the new academy was completed in 1933 it's predecessor became Shawlands Primary School. The pediments and decorative swags were lost when an extra storey was added in the 1930s.

STEVENSON DRIVE, SHAWLANDS, GLASGOW   (5)

Apart from the obvious name change, Deanston Drive has scarcely altered in the eighty odd years since this postcard was produced. Its residents, however, undoubtedly slept better than their modern counterparts, untroubled by the electronic ullulations of car alarms that never seem to be absent from this street today!

Neale Thomson of Camphill House bought the neighbouring estate of Langside in 1852, with the intention of creating a suburb of villas. In fact only two were ever built, and it was not until the 1870s that developers began to take an interest in the district. The village of Langside had existed in 1568, and it is believed that the scarcity of relics from the battle was caused by the inhabitants gathering any discarded metal from the field for scrap. The cottages in this 1906 picture dated from the early 18th century, and stood on the east side of Algie Place. They were the last survivors of the rural village, and were torn down around 1910.

Langside Battlefield Memorial & Victoria Infirmary, Glasgow.   72785 JV.

The Battle of Langside monument was erected by public subscription, and completed in 1888. The architect was Alexander Skirving who also designed the Langside Old Parish Church, which can be seen behind the monument in this Edwardian view. When it was opened for worship, this church was described as one of the most beautiful gothic churches in Glasgow. In recent years it was used by the Victoria Infirmary to store records, but was demolished in 1982 after it was gutted in a spectacular blaze.

Victoria Infirmary, Langside, Glasgow

Although the plans for the Victoria Infirmary were drawn up in 1882, construction did not begin for another six years. The architects were the firm of Campbell, Douglas and Sellars. The first part of the building to be completed was the administration block and former nurses' home, on the left of this 1905 postcard. On the facade of this building are carved the arms of Queen Victoria and a puma, incongruously representing "medical care".

Boys' Brigade Inspection at Glasgow,
27th April, 1912.

LORD INVERCLYDE.

EARL SHAFTESBURY.

SIR WILLIAM SMITH.
(FOUNDER OF BOY'S BRIGADE)

This 1912 postcard was published by the Glasgow firm of Millar and Lang. Their former factory still stands at the corner of Darnley Street and Albert Drive in Pollokshields. From 1904 until the late 1970s they were one of the largest Scottish manufacturers of greetings cards, and comic and view postcards. Their comprehensive captioning of the card has left the author little to add, except to provide the location which was the Queen's Park Recreation Ground. Prospecthill Terrace in Mount Florida can be seen in the background.